T0198422

Blu Wave Pearce, B.Ed., MA

To order additional copies of this book, contact:
Xlibris
844-714-8691
www.Xlibris.com
Orders@Xlibris.com

ISBN: Softcover   978-1-6641-8059-8
         EBook   978-1-6641-8058-1

Print information available on the last page

Rev. date: 06/21/2021

A special thanks goes out to
Kyle McDonald for all his help and ideas.

Dedicated to my first grandson, Gannon Christopher, my boys, Marc Christopher, Kyle Chance, and DustinJohn Howard, as well as, my family and friends who have supported me with my book.

is for

Armadillo

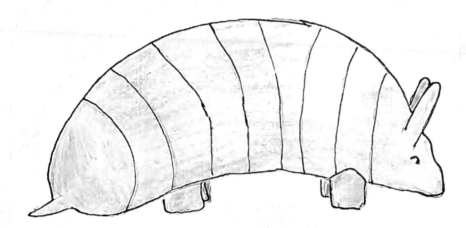

and has

Lifespan: 12-15yrs
Size: 5.9 - 9.8 inches
Weight: 5.5 - 73 lbs
Found: Native to
the Americas

is for

Beaver

and has

Lifespan: up to 10yrs
Size: 2.4 - 3.3 feet
Weight: 24 - 71 lbs
Found: Canada,
France, Germany,
North America,
Poland, Russia,
and Scandinavia

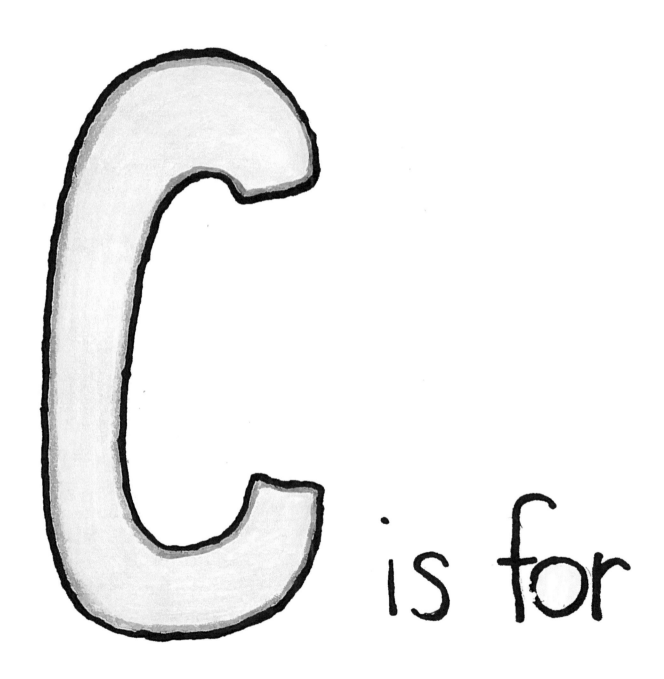

is for

Capabyra

and has

Lifespan: 10yrs
Size: 20-25 inches
Weight: 77-150lbs
Found: South
America

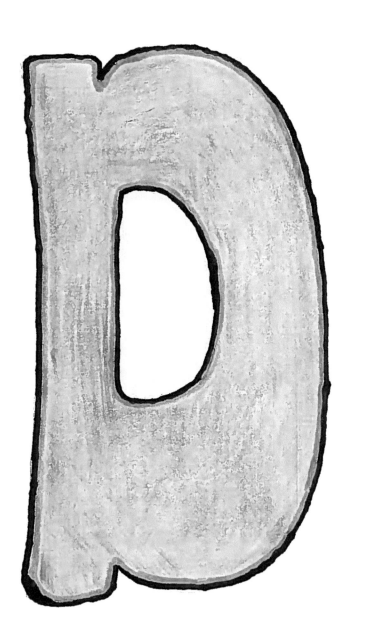

is for

Dolphin

and has

Lifespan: 40-60yrs
Size: 12.5feet
Weight: 330-1,400 lbs
Found: Worldwide

E is for

Eagle

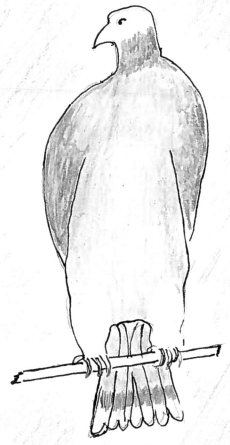

and has

Lifespan: 14-20 yrs
Size: 2.2 - 3.4 feet
Weight: 6.6 - 20 lbs
Found: Canda to
Mexico

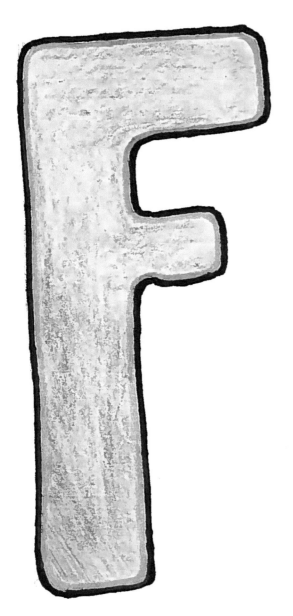

is for

Flamingo

and has

Lifespan: 40-60yrs
Size: 2.6-4.8feet
Weight: 4.4-8.8lbs
Found: on every
Continent except
Australia and
Antarctica

is for

Gorilla

and has

Lifespan: 35-40 yrs
Size: 5.1-6 feet
Weight: 330-350 lbs
Found: Sub-Saharan Africa

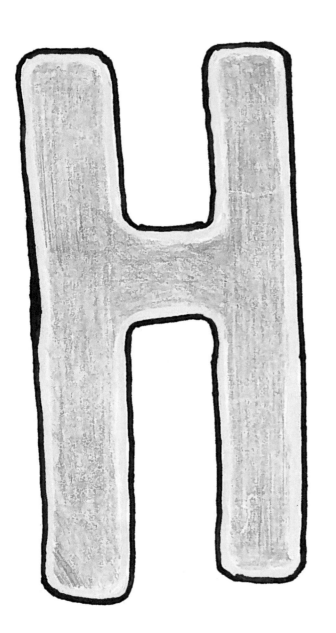

is for

Hyena

and has

Life span: up to 12 yrs
Size: 2-3 feet
Weight: 49-140 lbs
Found: Africa
and Asia

is for

Impala

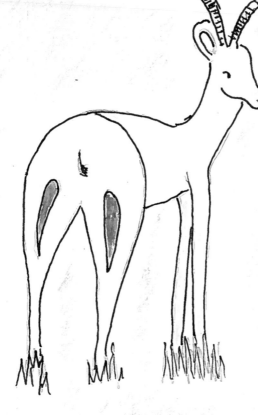

and has

Lifespan: up to 25.6 yrs
Size: 4 feet
Weight: 66 - 170 lbs
Found: Africa

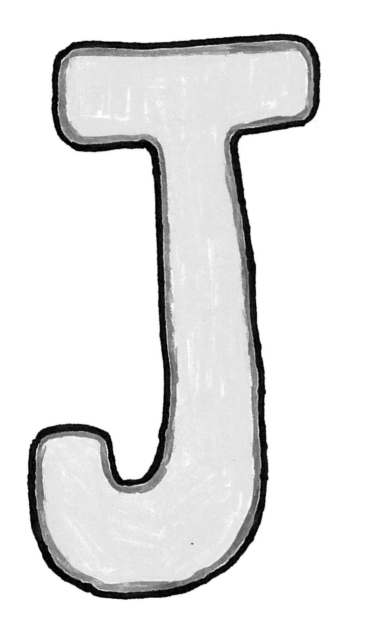

is for

Jackrabbit

and has

Lifespan: 18 mths-5 yrs
Size: 56-65 cm
Weight: 3.3-15 lbs
Found: Arctic,
Western United
States and Mexico

K

is for

Kangaroo

and has

Lifespan: up to 10 yrs
Size: up to 9.2 feet
Weight: 100-150 lbs
Found: Australia
and New Guinea

is for

Lemur

and has

Lifespan: 16-19 yrs
Size: 15 inches-4 feet
Weight: 4.9-19 lbs
Found: Native to Madagascar

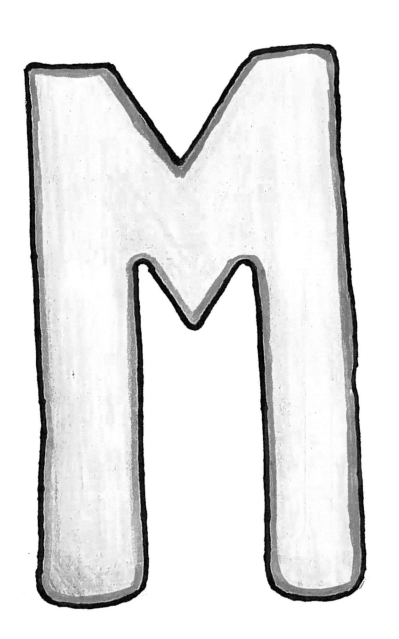

is for

Manatee

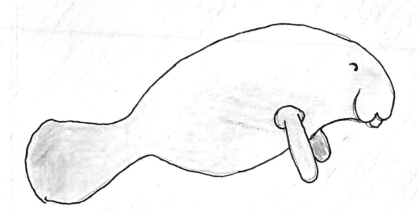

and has

Lifespan: up to 60 yrs
Size: 9-11 feet
Weight: 910-1,000 lbs
Found: Gulf of
Mexico, Amazon,
West African and
Indian Oceans

is for

Ningaui

and has

Lifespan: 12-14 mths
Size: 58-75 mm long
Weight: .22-3.3 ozs
Found: Australia

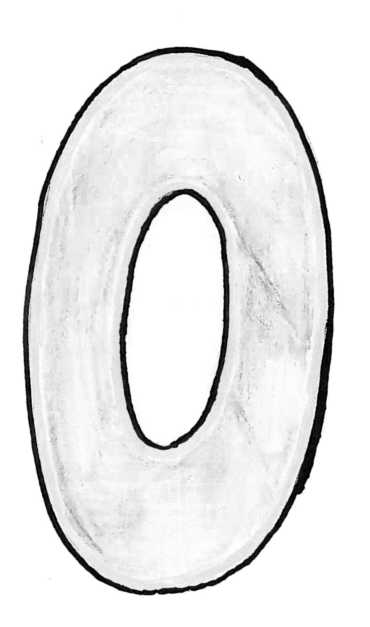

is for

Ostrich

and has

Lifespan: 50-75yrs
Size: 6.9-9.2feet
Weight: 140-320lbs
Found: Africa
and Asia Minor

is for

Platypus

and has

Lifespan: up to 17 yrs
Size: 17-20 inches
Weight: 1.5-5.3 lbs
Found: Australia
including Tasmania

is for

Quokka

and has

Lifespan: up to 10 yrs
Size: 25.8 - 32.8 inches
Weight: 2.5 - 6.7 lbs
Found: Island
off Western
Australia

is for

Rhinoceros

and has

Lifespan: 35-50 yrs
Size: 5.3-6.3 feet
Weight: 4,900-5,100 lbs
Found: Africa and Asia

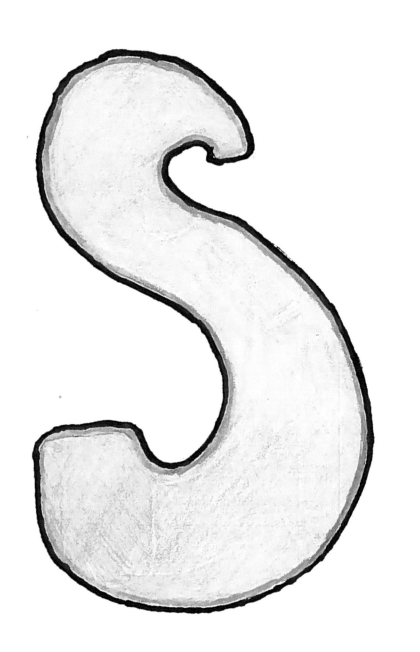

is for

Seahorse

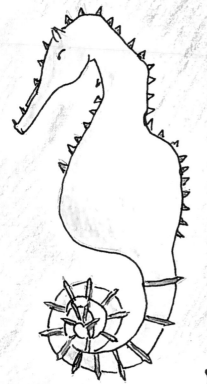

and has

Lifespan: 1-4yrs
Size: ½ - 14inches
Weight: 7oz - 1lb
Found: Temperate
and Tropical Oceans
Worldwide

T

is for

Tapir

and has

Lifespan: 25-30 yrs
Size: 3.3 feet
Weight: 330-350 lbs
Found: Central
and South America
and High Andes
Mountains

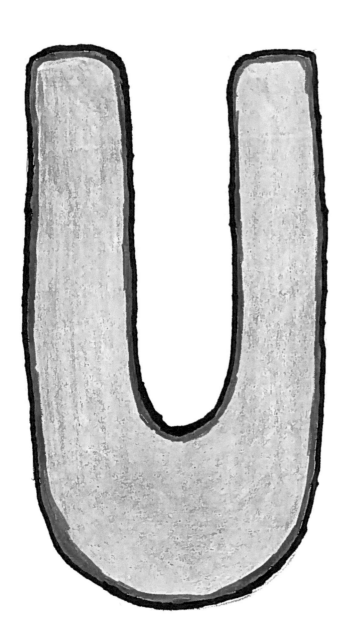

is for

Urchin

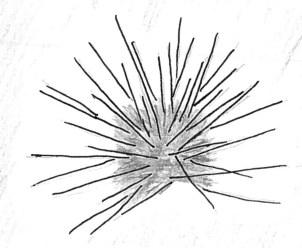

and has

Lifespan: up to 100yrs
Size: 6inch diameter
Weight: 1 lb
Found: in the
oceans worldwide

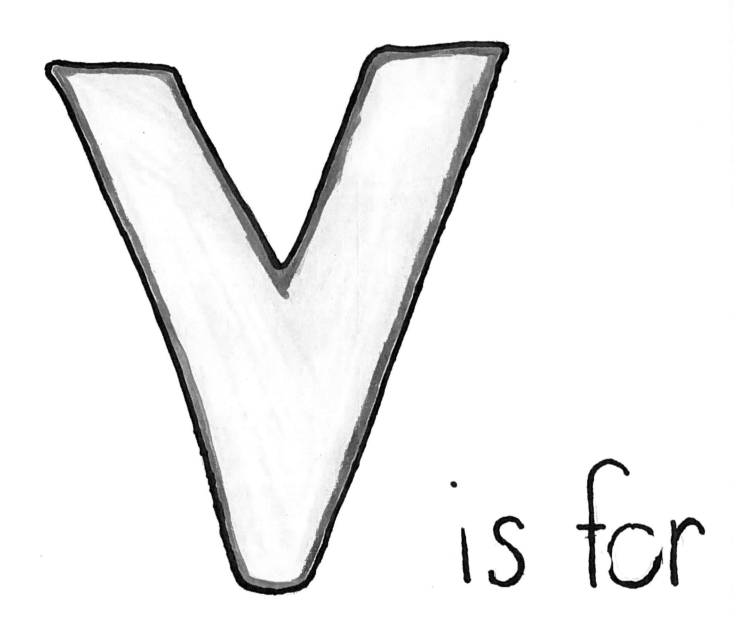

is for

Vicuna

and has

Lifespan: 15-20yrs
Size: 2.5-2.8feet
Weight: 77-140lbs
Foud: Argentina,
Bolivia, Chili, Peru,
and Equador

is for

Walrus

and has

Lifespan: up to 40 yrs
Size: 12 feet long
Weight: 2,200 lbs
Found: North Pole
in the Arctic Ocean
and the Northern
Hemisphere

is for

Xenops

and has

Lifespan: 9-10.5yrs
Size: 12cm
Weight: 12grams
Found: Southern
Mexico, South to
Western Ecuador

is for

Yak

and has

Lifespan: 20+yrs
Size: 3.4-4.5 feet
Weight: 500-1,300lbs
Found: Himalayas,
Mongolia, Siberia,
and Tibetan
Plateau

is for

Zokor

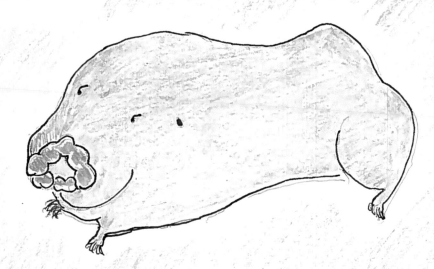

and has

Lifespan: 1 – 4.5 yrs
Size: 6-10 inches long
Weight: 5-20 ounces
Found: North Asia

References

https://actionchange.org
https://www.activewild.com
https://alphabetimals.com
https://www.allaboutbirds.com
https://animalcorner.org
https://www.animals.net
https://animaldiversity.org
https://www.aviary.org
https://animalia.bio
https://www.biologicaldiversity.org
https://arctickingdom.com
https://www.britannica.com
https://arvi.google.com
https://www.elephants.com
https://a-z-animals.com
https://www.google.com
https://bioone.org
https://www.humanesociety.org
https://birdsoftheworld.org
https://www.lifescience.com
https://cradlepoint.com
https://www.livescience.com
https://elephantaidinternational.org
https://www.merriam-webster.cocm
https://en.m.wikipedia.org
https://www.mspca.org
https://eol.org

https://www.nationalgeographic.com
https://facts.carolinaraptorcenter.org
https://www.nature.com
https://infovisual.info
https://www.owlresearchinstitute.org
https://justfunfacts.com
https://www.researchgate.net
https://kids.kindle.co
https://www.shutterstock.com
https://ocean.si.edu
https://www.thoughtco.com
https://oceana.org
https://www.treehugger.com
https://onekindplanet.org
https://www.trunksnleaves.org
https://pubmed.ncbi.nim.nih.gov
https://www.visionsoftheworld.org
https://sciencing.com
https://www.visitsealife.com
https://search.app.goo.gl
https://www.wwf.org.uk
https://study.com
https://www.zoology.vbc.ca
https://trishansoz.com
https://us.whales.org
https://visualdictionary.org

Printed in the United States
by Baker & Taylor Publisher Services